THE FLAME

PRAISE FOR SUHAIL MIRZA'S POETRY AND SPIRITUAL
WRITING FROM AROUND THE WORLD

———

Suhail Mirza is a Modern day Rumi! His Poetry takes you to a place of unconditional Love and passion that everyone deserves to have! Suhail's poetry touches me on a very deep level and he writes it straight from his beautiful heart!!!!

Lisa Ferrin, Redondo Beach, California, USA

Suhail Mirza is The Twin Flame divinely channeled Poet. Period. That his magnificently Divine poetry is reminiscent of the great poet Rumi is no coincidence!

Buttercup Lawson Meyer, Miami, USA

Suhail Mirza's poetry reveals a depth of love that is unique. His words touch the deepest recesses of the heart and take you on a mystical journey to a realm where love itself resides.

Veronica Forster, Melbourne, Australia

Suhail is a true romantic. His vivid and beautiful poetry makes me remember the strength and dignity to be found within and how love shines a light into the darkest hours.

Verity Buchanan, London, UK

Suhail's poetry gets to the heart of unconditional love, the balance of the Divine Feminine and Masculine and captures the true spirit of our era. His words inspire us all to heal, love and grow deeper.

Pilar Stella, Venice Beach, CA, USA

There are some people who are 'born writers' – it is these people who have that unique gift of being able to take the inner and deepest emotions experienced by human beings and articulate them into words... consequently, Suhail's poetry speaks to your soul, providing it with a platform to express those feelings that we often don't have the words to describe.

Dr Karan Jutlla, Birmingham, UK

Suhail's writing is a spiritual breeze of beautiful, heartfelt and inspiring words that transcend the soul.

Isabel Puente, La Corunna, Spain

I love to read every single word of Suhail's writing. It is gorgeous. His words deeply impact my heart. His spiritual poetry transforms and is full of love and light.

Carmen Scherer, Lake Constance, Germany

Prose that has been weaved with emotions, passion, love and cosmic secrets. A delight to read, an adventure to experience!

Nida K., Washington DC, USA

Suhail's poetry will spark your imagination; His words unveil the infinite space where lovers' passion cannot be contained.

AJ Beaber, Texas, USA

Suhail's poetry inspires at a heart and soul level with a voice much like Rumi or Hafiz. I feel the LOVE he writes, is the Divine's gift to those who commit to living in authenticity, right action, and genuine connection with the Divine. Suhail's poetry gives us a glimpse of our Divine gift.

Alexandra Sofia, Malibu, California, USA

Suhail writes absolutely beautiful love poems. Each phrase of his poetry is saturated full of deep meaning. Each one romantic, touching, emotional, and captivating. These are the emotions that arise when I read each poem.

Guzyal Nurmagambetova, Aktau, Kazakhstan

Suhail's poetry makes my mind relax and get lost in what is the essence of the Divine; Love. I look forward to reading every one of his poems and connecting with the words that allow me to open my heart.

Leigh Marie, London, UK

Suhail's poems offer peace so deep it transforms into a physical feeling in my chest. Helping to observe change with intuition.

Natalie Wright, Brisbane, Australia

Suhail's poetry fuses intellect and emotion in a high and noble human experience. From Poet to paper and paper to Poet. I thank him for sharing the depth of his heart.

Wyn Duraes, London, UK

Suhail has an incredible way with words. His ability to talk about themes of love, truth and vulnerability in a way that is easily digestible and relatable to all age groups is second to none. When you read his work, it feels as if he is speaking directly to you. This can only be done by someone who has gone through a journey themselves and has the courage to bare their soul to help benefit others with the things they have learned.

Megha Kumar, London, UK

Love is the most powerful and indestructible force in the entire universe. Suhail Mirza has the great fortune of being blessed in transforming it into words of beautiful poetry.

Marta Irene Guagliana, Mar del Plata, Argentina

Reading Suhail Mirza's poetry is to enter in a magical world of love and fly in the serenity of his words. Suhail's work reveals the true essence of life; we are here just for a short time and his writing offers us the suggestion how to live this time in an authentic and better way!

Luciano Mucelli, Carpaneto, Italy

Suhail's beautiful words capture everyone's heart. He is reviving Poetry which has been endangered especially through his theme of "Twin Flame Poetry".I find his poems exquisite always giving excitement and happiness that touches my heart.

Eleanor S.Ibasco, Lucena City, Philippines

On first reading Suhail's poetry I understood the work to be purely about romantic love. But when I applied it to my own journey of living my life authentically and as I truly desire, the meaning all fell into place for me. This poetry is relatable in whichever form to anyone, if they make it so.

Leigh Grassi, Birmingham U.K.

Each poem about love that Suhail writes fills me with hope and reminds me that the real purpose of life is to love first and beyond all else. Wisdom and strength are found in each line of poetry which Suhail carefully constructs with intent to divulge deep insight into the mysteries of life and love. His poems are reminiscent of the Persian Poet Rumi, but with a modern and extraordinarily romantic twist.

Susan Daniels, Oregon, USA

Suhail's poems create a fantastic enthusiasm in readers' minds for life and love. His words reveal one of the most pious souls whom I have ever encountered in my life.

Jai Gurudev, Ghaziabad, New Delhi, India

Suhail's authentically challenging poetry continues to inspire me to have the courage to continue journeying deeper within my limitless soul and to continue bringing forth my divine, untapped gifts.

Orlando W. Darden Jr, Washington, DC USA

Suhail's poems speak of magic and love. Words of Divinity that go deep and touch the heart and soul. A truly beautiful expression of the best that masculine energy can be.

Louise K. Taylor, Auckland, New Zealand

I am honoured to sing the praises of Suhail Mirza; this gifted heart-centred poet. Through his poems, he weaves a mystical gossamer fabric - blending the esoteric brilliance of a Rumi with the soul passions of a Vatsyayana.

Sara Thompson, Virginia, USA

The
FLAMES
of
LOVE

*Poems of the journey of
Divine Love*

Suhail Mirza

Matador
9 Priory Business Park,
Wistow Road, Kibworth Beauchamp,
Leicestershire. LE8 0RX
Tel: 0116 279 2299
Email: books@troubador.co.uk
Web: www.troubador.co.uk/matador
Twitter: @matadorbooks

ISBN 978 1789017 663

British Library Cataloguing in Publication Data.
A catalogue record for this book is available from the British Library.

Printed and bound in Great Britain by 4edge Limited
Typeset in 11pt Baskerville by Troubador Publishing Ltd, Leicester, UK

Matador is an imprint of Troubador Publishing Ltd

To Leilu

No longer the boy at the butcher's shop.
Thank you for bringing me home.

CONTENTS

THE ORIGIN OF
THE FLAMES OF LOVE

How my "dark night of the soul"
opened the Path of Love

How does a former lawyer, steeped in the modern Age which worships the rational and the worldly, become a mystical poet of love? Ultimately by being broken and having his heart shattered such that surrender to the Path of Love was the only option to save his spirit.

In my book " Many Mansions" I shared my journey from a place of desolation and despair to the reclamation of the Light that shines within each of us. It was a journey that brought me home ; to the Eternal that is our Origin and our Essence.

So many readers from around the world have been kind enough to contact me and say how the book has given them hope in their own times of crisis. These comments and the book's success (becoming a top three on Amazon's Spirituality listing) has been so humbling and nourishing to my soul.

Yet some readers have asked for the details about the "dark night of the soul" that lead to my transformative spiritual journey. At that time my book could not reveal this. However in honour to these requests, the imperative of self authenticity and due to profound changes in my own life I want now to unveil that truth; for it is from the Path of Love that poetry flowed.

While the suffering of an innocent initially prompted my crisis of Faith it was the betrayal of my heart, and particularly its aftermath, that was the "darkest night". That betrayal led to the breakdown of my marriage of many years and an emotional shattering as profound as I could have imagined. The depth of despair lead me to be broken at the core of my being. Even to my questioning my own value.

Yet at the moment when rationality might have insisted that I pull up the drawbridge to my heart in self preservation; my spiritual journey simply plunged me onto the Path of

Love. That path that lead me to break further the vessels of my heart and share the love within as fully as I possibly could. Ultimately in my personal life this has not lead to my marriage being saved, an outcome for which I had hoped, even amidst the pain of a broken heart.

Yet I would not turn back the hands of time. From the "hell" of that emotional shattering and desolation I found the "heaven" that is our true abode of existence. That "heaven" which transcends spatial and temporal boundaries. For that "heaven" is found within ourselves.

Through that darkest despair I was lead to the language of love. It was from that Path of Love that I was able to reclaim the Light that shines above and within.

I finally learned that I, like each of us, is beautiful and deserving of the Divine Love for which our heart perennially yearns in this created realm. No matter the pain and disappointments we have endured. Yet still we must seek that reunion with the twin with whom we stood in pre-eternity.

I do, however, confess that I remain humbled to find myself the conveyance for the poetry of Divine Love's journey. Yet I can see now that this was to be essential in honouring my reclamation of the exquisite balance of

Divine Femininity and Divine Masculinity which has a central place in Traditional Wisdom.

The poems have simply "revealed" themselves in visions of my heart and I have sought , no doubt imperfectly but sincerely, to capture the beauty of that Imaginal world in the words of each poem.

As the wonderful AJ Beaber states, in her gracious Foreword to this book, Love is Eternal and can never be extinguished. Ultimately it is the only true Reality. It is our true identity.

Suhail Mirza
London
October 2018

ABOUT
SUHAIL MIRZA

A few years ago Suhail was faced with a crisis of meaning and despite all the trappings of worldly success his despair lead him to question the value of his existence. Only when he rediscovered the timeless principles of Traditional Wisdom could his own personal transformation begin. This lead him to write the stunning spiritual guide, Many Mansions, a book loved by readers from around the world and which became a Top Three title in Amazon's spirituality charts.

His latest book, The Flames of Love, contains the poetry (likened by many to Rumi) of Divine Love. Suhail himself says the poems come from a heart that was plunged onto The Path of Love after experiencing the "deepest dark night of the soul" and an emotional shattering that threatened his very sense of self.

Suhail has been interviewed both live on BBC Radio London's Inspirit programme and also by BBC Radio Oxford about his mystical writing. He has also appeared on Alena Chapman's 30 Minute Moments radio show in the USA.

Suhail Mirza grew up in East London, graduated in Law from the London School of Economics and worked as an employment rights lawyer, where he represented those facing discrimination and unfair treatment in the workplace. He later went into recruitment, wrote the acclaimed book "Meet the CEO" and still serves as City Editor for the leading trade journal Recruitment International.

He is also founder of "Spiritual Solutions" a platform for anyone who, like him, is facing a crisis of meaning. The platform offers resources to undertake the same journey (from darkness to light) that Suhail has taken. He has also created an audio programme in which he personally takes people through each of the 10 steps of "The Spiritual Solution" and his journey.

Suhail divides his time between Kent (the Garden of England) and London. He has also spent much time in Andalusia which he describes as his "spiritual home".

FOREWORD

This book will spark your imagination;
The infinite space where lovers' passion cannot be contained

By AJ Beaber

"There are still those of us that recall a different time; when promises
made were meant to abide. When simply the glimpse of a woman's
eyes remained a man's greatest prize... When to honour, cherish and
adore her, was what men understood love was meant for."

- Suhail Mirza, The Flames of Love

Suhail's poetry is written for the lover inside all. Suhail
has journeyed to the secret garden where the Divine
Masculine and Feminine rejoice, in union, ignited by the
celebration of their love. And has returned to share his
poetic findings here in The Flames of Love.

Using the language of the lovers, Suhail's poetry conveys
that this secret garden is not an ephemeral fairy tale; rather

it exists in the space between, which resides within us all. Where the great love story lives on, to ignite our own.

In my experience of Suhail's writing I continue to expand in the appreciation of my own Divine Masculine. I find healing and anointing for the scars of my earthly relationships. I am reminded where the flames of true love reside, knowing that this love is eternal, and can never be extinguished. And through Suhail's honouring of the Divine Feminine, I find safety and permission to honour my own, with every reading, strengthening this relationship in the external.

This poetry is more than words. For those who are open, it is an opportunity to reunite with your beloved, over and over again. Nourished by Suhail's translation, this book will spark your imagination; the infinite space where lovers' passion cannot be contained.

Burning in purity, passion and possibility within these Flames of Love.

Thank you Suhail for this beautiful Gift.

AJ Beaber, Author of You and I Inc
Public Speaker and Founder of Ignite the Light
Dallas, Texas, USA

PART I

Preparation

REMEMBRANCE

All journeys to the summit of Divine Love and its reunion commence within our hearts. At this moment. At this place. At this stage in our life. If we are prepared to surrender.

Traditional Wisdom speaks of a time where humanity once thought with the Mind of Heaven and moved with the Breathe of the Divine. Time has passed so much that today we are inveighed to look only with physical eyes; no longer able to discern the signs. That once lifted us beyond the physical; that once made us intimate with the Spiritual.

Only in the dreams of a polished heart can we again start our return above. Where in our silence resides the Language of love.

Today the search for significance has perhaps never been greater; yet so many forage for fortune, fame or favour. In what is the external. But that which is Eternal remains present in every atom of Creation. Awaiting our reclamation.

Traditional Wisdom teaches us that those who truly know themselves shall thereby truly know their Lord. So fellow traveller, commence your search anew; don't look out there, for all Truth resides in you.

Our Greatest Test

Long ages have passed since our time in Celestial Bliss
That abode of peace which each human heart does miss

Our created world though beautifully full of splendour
Remains a veil to the Light which strives to always render

The language of heaven to this world accessible
Yet relying upon only our minds, a task impossible

Only when we can venture into that world of Imagination
That communes with the realms of Heaven and Creation

Will we see beyond External Forms to their true nature
And our soul shall bear witness in all its rapture

That forever we each carry Heaven's Truth in our breast
That opening our hearts remains this life's greatest test

Our True Disposition

All true knowledge is wisdom recollected
Ours is a vast heritage not one confected

From the deceit of modernism's curse
Which sees only a pitiless purposeless universe

And humanity as simply unintended accidents
With lives nasty brutish & without consequence

Yet in the depths of our hearts we must know
That the language of Heaven will always show

Us the path that will return us to that mystical land
Where each soul by its Angel was taken by the hand

To that Truth forever bathed in Divine Compassion
That Love shall forever be our true disposition

Our Greatest Liberation

Should we seek to escape the shadows of our past
How to remember the answers to the questions Destiny asked?

Condemned to repeat the errors of ignorance
From whence would we find our deliverance?

Be not bereft; for Heaven assures our path
Reminding us that it's Mercy outweighs its Wrath

Provided we are prepared to offer true contrition
For each error, each action and each omission

That which was opaque within shall become clear
Igniting the light of Faith we can banish our fear

And in offering sincere witness and confession
Find that the truth gives our greatest liberation

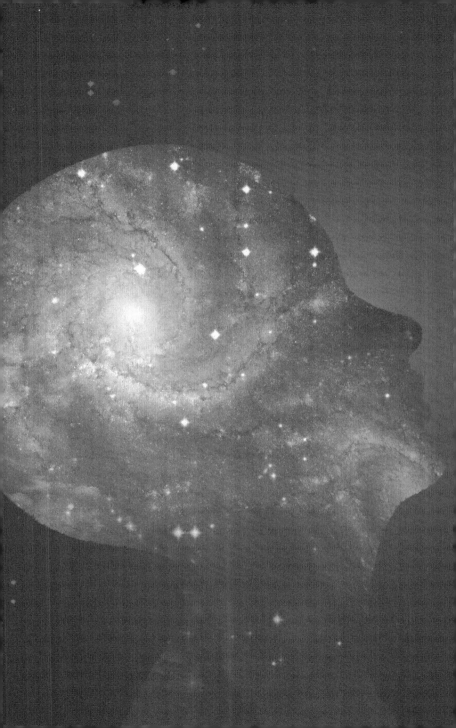

Darkness and Light

Upon what horizon should we gaze if we yearn
For that freedom only our heart can discern?

Should we see only the outward forms of Life
We may drown in images of conflict and strife

Yet polishing our heart we can open its eyes
And have unveiled all of Heaven's signs

Of the timeless wisdom ordering all of Creation
Of our humanity as the Divine's great emanation

For in our inner ascension we seek annihilation
In order to shed illusion to attain our True station

Where once again we can dance in His Sight
And transcend the duality of darkness and light

Love's Dwelling

In each authentic Man's heart nostalgia seeks that abode
Far from this madding world where Men's souls are sold

In that pursuit within the Reign of Quantity
Where even intimacy is reduced to commodity

Man now justifies his lower lust within a number
Exonerating his abuse and failing to remember

His true nature as the Regent of Heavenly Light
In his forgetfulness plunged into an endless night

Traditional Wisdom offers paths to regain spiritual sight
The whispers of the human heart knows what is right

That in loving his beloved he creates a vision Divinely compelling

That in uniting his heart to hers he creates Love's Eternal Dwelling

Paradox of Peace

When at last our life's destination here we reach
Shall we be able to recall its lessons to teach?

What shall be the story our epitaph shall tell
Did we make of our life a heaven or a hell?

Were we courageous bearing love's most painful stings
Marvelling still at the miracle each new sunrise brings?

In the extremities of life could we still find our centre
Cleaving to love; striving to make others' lives better?

Forlorn are those who limit this world to what they know
Wisdom demands that always our hearts' love must flow

So that it's light shines forever even as life must cease
In our strength and surrender rests the paradox of peace

Our True Home

We who have existed among the shadows
Have paid that price which our heart knows

Into bondage we fell; seeking the allure of freedom
In our slumber we traded hell for our mighty kingdom

Forlorn we became; of ever escaping this cage
Ceaselessly tearful prose filling our every page

Only turning up to Heaven did we begin to learn
That His Beloved Mercy every pure heart can earn

Through sincere witness to our manifold mistakes
The Grace of forgiveness ensures Heaven never forsakes

Any heart surrendered truly to Love alone
His Light surely can guide us to our true home

Love's Glance

We who seek still to clothe our lives in eternal verity
See so many who regard honour as no longer a necessity

In a world where shallowness is deified
Miraculous that even a few "old souls" have survived

To carry the torch of Truth and ignite its light
To be warriors in this last phase of the Divine fight

For those whose suffering can seem ceaseless
In a world which Modernism teaches is pitiless

Must be reminded of their beautiful self worth
Each and every one Heaven's Viceregent on Earth

For every soul perennially deserves the chance
To be bathed in the beauty of Love's eternal glance

Unveil the Light

Should we fear the sound of our silence
Have we forgotten the time of our innocence?

When our true nature was our only conveyance
That time when even darkness was held in abeyance?

Yet indeed our world has become broken
Too many now treat Love as a mere token

We who are witness to this inversion
Need not however look away in aversion

For we each carry the torch of truth; here
Within our breast, where love can slay fear

Now is that hour not for flight but to fight
Now is that moment to Unveil our Light

One Embrace

Today ever more we see in each other a stranger
Unaware that this carries the gravest danger

Of rendering within humanity division and hate
Vacuous leaders already claim conflict is our fate

Late is the hour within this duel with darkness
Yet together we still can overcome forgetfulness

For we can all recall our unity before our Fall
Will we now have the courage to answer the call?

To proclaim that Oneness remains Faith's essence
That Unity of Being resides in every human soul's quintessence

That we should see ourselves reflected in every strangers face
That we can share all the Love of Heaven in just One Embrace

BALANCE

To whom does a Man bear witness in his soul; To whom does he call in his travels?

Traditional Wisdom unveils the Truth that in the Face of Woman is reflected all the potentialities of Heaven's Beauty.

Only that Man who suspends time in her eyes; places all Faith in her touch and all Heaven in her kiss can truly gain his Truth. For it is in such moments of intense "marital union" that the veils are torn asunder and Man confronts his peace in such surrender.

The Masculine and Feminine are garments of Light made for one another. Each other's beloved, far indeed they have traveled together. In those realms whence they came to find rest. Ordained to have their love put to life's test.

Should the Masculine not place the Feminine upon a pedestal reaching into the sky? A summit he may never reach no matter how hard he might try. Or should he confine her to this realm on Earth? Into that endless dance between death and rebirth?

Better that the truly Masculine Man wish to be separated from her; Than to limit her Wisdom to only that which he knows to be true. For in the Divine Feminine is the heart of the Angel of Light. Whose luminosity would overwhelm his sight.

Yet he does yearn, to earn, her trust and still burn; with all his Masculine desire, to see their flames of love once again become One Fire.

Divine Feminine

Once more we must light the candle of our vigil
Praying that even now there remains time still

To reverse our world which has fallen inside out
We whose hearts know truth must learn to shout

The name of Wisdom itself; Sophia, Sophia !
In her reclamation our hope that the Light will reappear

That light that shone upon us all in pre-eternity
Which our Modernism seeks to consign to mere mythology

Yet she is the Soul of our World; our Angel of Countenance
Only in communion with her can our hearts see the
Divine's Immanence

Only in the true adoration of Woman can Man again begin
His journey to the Divine in the heart of the Feminine

Love's Resurrector

Should true Masculinity be eclipsed in our Age of Decline
Whence should true Femininity turn to again find?

That Man for whom chivalry is worth every sacrifice
For whom nothing less than Divine Honour shall suffice

We who still believe in such values must remain resolute
In our words and deeds the lie of Modernism refute

For this Man, my Angel, bares his soul before you
Asking only Time be the arbiter of whether he is true

In his promise to make your adoration his core mission
In his promise to find heaven in your every contradiction

Awed by you, forever he wishes to be your protector
Burning all veils, he offers his life as Love's Resurrector

Love for All Seasons

We who remember the innocence of earlier days
Still believe that our heart knows many ways

To express its truth; though only adoration of the Feminine
Can truly permit any fallen man to once again begin

To trust that tomorrow is best left to Destiny
To trust that yesterday is now simply a Memory

And that in this moment all lives are renewed
For the Feminine is a heart with Divine Love imbued

My beloved; will you lift your veils of self protection?
So your soul can see my heart's true intention

And find that this man begs to give you all reasons
To know that his adoration is for all love's seasons

Love's Incandescence

In my dreams we still walk upon still waters
Placing bouquets of Love upon Heaven's altars

Would that I could make each dream last forever
No earthly peace compares to souls united together

Yet sojourn I must upon a world ablaze in conflict
Seeking still an oasis of peace that may subsist

In you, my Angel, my heart recapitulates it's claims
Only the Feminine the roar of Masculinity tames

In her compassion she is the epiphany of Divine Mercy
In her tenderness she tempers Divine Majesty

In her eyes Man finds immanence and Transcendence
In her heart, Man is enflamed by Love's Incandescence

Love's Symphony

Long years have passed since our Second Birth
Awakened we have sought that Light on Earth

That illumined the Souls of Men in Ancient Days
Now attenuated in shadows in manifold ways

Yet burning still within every authentic Man's breast
That Truth to which his heart must always attest

Such that without his Twin his soul screams in silence
Bereft and broken it recalls its lost innocence

My Angel, I have searched for you in every Age
You are the music written on my heart's every page

Heaven's Merciful Light unveiled my Life's Epiphany
The beating of our hearts is Love's Sacred Symphony

Love's Angel

We who feel incomplete still strive to seek
That Unity far from a world in full retreat

Whose embrace in our Creation still envelops
Our soul as it's purification ceaselessly develops

In order that it may be worthy of her grace
To bear witness to the beauty within her face

For all is unfolding in alignment with Divine Fate
The honourable heart yearns always for its mate

My beloved, the signs have revealed my Celestial Twin
Redeemed, discarding dishonour, so that I may begin

To surrender my heart to that which is truly Eternal
To pledge my soul to you forever, Love's True Angel

Love's Consummation

Think not that that Time of Angels has on Earth ceased
We ,whose eyes are open, walk toward the spiritual feast

That is laid upon the Heavenly Table of Ultimate Unity
Celebrating our betrothal in that fabled Sapphire City

Atop the sacred Mountain whose path is revealed
For those whose hearts remain brave and never sealed

But open in surrender in search of our true reflection
Masculinity knows in the Feminine resides his perfection

This sacred balance in all Wisdom's texts finds mention
Whose truth is our protection until the Final Resurrection

My Angel I offer my heart in quivering supplication
Let us unite and melt in Love's eternal Consummation

Love's Pure Gaze

We fall to our knees in prayer to reclaim our mission
And thus to honour our primordial Celestial position

In our remembrance of the wisdom of the Angel of Light
She who lifts our souls; who gives our hearts sight

She is the daughter of the Infinite; the dwelling of All
She bathed us in Mercy in that moment before our Fall

Man can all the world conquer yet still be meek
His heart shall not know peace until her we seek

Ours is the dominion and regency of the Earth
Yet our true kingship begins in our second birth

To our Divine Feminine whence Creation shall commence
a new phase

As the dwelling of truth bathed in the light of Love's
pure gaze

Love's Source

We whose soul has journeyed to many stations
Have in our aloneness rested with great patience

For that unveiling with which all our pretence
Is cast aside, revealing only our essence

Teaching us the Feminine is the ground of all creation
In her receptive beauty alone can man seek ascension

To his higher self, his true mode of being
For the polished heart alone is all seeing

Such that in you, my beloved, lies Heaven's reflection
Such that in you is revealed Divinity's Perfection

Such that my heart asks yours to direct its course
Such that my heart sees your light as love's source

Love made Infinite

Oftentimes I cannot believe one such as you
Exists in this world today, where now so few

Believe in that Heavenly balance of Masculinity and
Femininity
Ordained by the Creative Wisdom for all of Eternity

Through your presence every facet of my heart
Finds its authentic expression and plays its part

Such that I can adore you with the tenderness of a poet's touch
Such that even igniting my warrior's passion is never too much

And find paradise as my fingers begin to trace
Every beautiful contour of your wonderful face

For you are my Divine Goddess made incarnate
In you I can at last see how Love is made Infinite

PART II

The Journey

HEARTBREAK

Some will dishonour you; some will seek to diminish You. Others will denigrate your beauty. Imperfection is a fact of this realm; the sinister sits aside the sublime. The cruel with the compassionate.

Fortunate are those who find their essence in that which is eternal within; who travel to their hearts and replenish that which has been taken. In times of ease offer part of your prayers and joy to others who are suffering; for perhaps it was such strangers' prayers that helped our healing.

In our tears of compassion there is a sign; that Heaven's Light resides within during each moment in time.

We who have been scarred; have still to journey far. Beyond the shadows left by those we embraced; even as we were left alone, our sorrows to face.

For we who love "too much" must honour the call to always lead with that love. Provided we also respect every other emotion; so the world knows we can never be broken.

Our compassion must never be confused with being weak; is it not written that the world belongs to the meek? So let us surrender our heart in vulnerability; and rediscover our heroism in our Fated ability to love for Eternity.

The Pain of Memory

We who wear our hearts upon our sleeve
Cling with all our might to still believe

In the redemptive power of love's presence
In the vision we carry within our essence

That one day the Pain we bear shall be extinguished
Such that our existence is no longer anguished

By the recollection of those whose darkness
Of heart, rendered us enveloped in emptiness

In faith we seek our refuge and transformation
In that Divine Love of which we are an emanation

Such is the true path to reclaim our destiny
Where our love erases the pain of memory

Ocean without a Shore

Long are the years since our tears were shed
Perhaps our doubt left so many words unsaid

Memory however persists; seeking to capture
Those moments that were shared in rapture

Yet better I never forget the depths of sorrow
To inform my present for a better tomorrow

For surely that day will dawn;
when I am again born and my Spirit no longer torn

Between what I was once and who I am now
In order that, at long last, my heart will allow

It's flame of love to blaze fully once more
And live it's truth as an Ocean without a Shore

Love's Reflection

Would that I could unwind the procession of Time
And once again that land of innocent hearts find

Where kindred souls unbound by the whims of Fate
Could their truths to each other fulsomely state

Yet in this world of imperfection we must sojourn
Knowing that at times our tender hearts will be broken

Between epochs of Light and darkness we must dance
Within the vision that one day may come our chance

To once more take the hand of our beloved Twin
And plunge into that Divine sacred stream to swim

Toward the Heavenly Spring, the source of all Creation
In its waters see in each other, Love's eternal reflection

Love's Youthfulness

Years weigh upon the soul that seeks release
From a worldly bondage; beckoning toward peace

Diminished we have allowed ourselves to become
Only by shedding our veils have we at last begun

To trace the tracks of the tears we have shed
To recall how often in pain our heart has bled

Yet still we cleaved to that yearning long unabated
Knowing only in the Eternal will our heart be satiated

You my Angel have turned back the hands of Time
Allowing my heart to see where once it was blind

Within each other's eyes we unearth truthfulness
Within our hearts we forever reclaim love's youthfulness

Love's Tenderness

Should we regret that our hearts were shattered
That our dreams and hopes strewn in tatters?

Should we suppress the memory of our weeping
Discard the depths of despair we were feeling?

To grasp respite from the shadows of the past
To wrestle an escape even after the die is cast?

No, my Angel, the call of Heaven rings loudly within
Still propelling me toward you, In order to begin

That journey to the centre of my true Essence
Where from pre eternity has resided your presence

The touch of your lips erases all life's bitterness
The light in your eyes unlocks Love's eternal tenderness

Love Enduring

Much we have suffered; oppression by convention
And empty rituals slay even the purest Intention

Yet I am not those Men; who dishonour Faith
For my heart overflows with love not hate

I have walked the path of fire and survived
Only when broken did I know I had arrived

To learn that to be your rock through all Time
I had to surrender and be vulnerable enough to find

The Light you ignited within me in those Ancient days
When we learned to share our love in infinite ways

In my dreams that memory is ceaselessly reappearing
Beckoning me to you once more; to love forever enduring

Love's Endlessness

Should we remember those times we were bereft
Shattered when destiny decreed love had left

Ours is the comfort to know that our hearts were true
A confession sought by many but deserved by so few

Time pursues it's desire to reach that point of peace
When it's constant unfolding shall finally cease

When my Angel ,our souls meet, Time's march we arrest
Infinity can be glimpsed within the love filled breast

Betrothed from pre-eternity your place is in my heart
It matters not when in Time's cycle our truth should start

We have danced forever in the realms of timelessness
Ours already a fabled story of Love's Endlessness

Your Tears

My love is yours for every single season
My heart's adoration yours for every reason

Our paths entwined to make you mine
Your heart the greatest treasure I could find

Yet I feel the wounds within your memory
Each a part of your very special destiny

For I too have tasted that dark night
When even hope seemed a distant light

Until I broke the vessels of my heart to release
The truth of love which leads to our peace

For you I shall confront every one of your fears
For you I shall offer to cry every one of your tears

Pain as my Friend

Words now fail me whenever I envision you
With each touch, each kiss I am born anew

Should I dampen my ardour for each embrace
Seek to limit my awe at the beauty of your face?

Yet this would dishonour the name of Love
Whose essence emanates from Heaven above

So I offer you my passion and my prose
Every heart must reap what it sows

For you my Angel of Beauty saved my soul
Destiny decreed for your compassion this role

With you true love began and with you it shall end
In bringing us together pain became my friend

Love's Sacred Trust

Should we once more stand at Love's crossroads
Would we hesitate to journey within its many abodes

For that union whose promise remains unfulfilled
Drowned by life's noise we yearn for waters stilled

Seeking reclamation of dreams disappointment has killed
To plant again seeds of hope in land so often tilled

Overcome we must such memories that make us weep
Every breathtaking summit's path is necessarily steep

Reminded by the vision of our Angel through the haze
Now is the hour of freedom from our heartbreak's maze

And so clasp our beguiling Angel's hand we must
And so surrender our heart to Love's sacred Trust

YEARNING

That which is below cannot be identical to that which is above ; a true friend cannot be our foe. That which is wrong cannot be equal to that which is right; the Heavenly Scale weighs all.

We can only find ourselves before our Fall; if we reveal all, of our heart to those who share it.

Love can only arise when "like meets like"; soul melts into soul, when two hearts truly become Light upon Light.

We shall then meet in the sapphire sea of the mystics and saints; in our dreams and higher states. Shedding the cloak placed upon us long ago; in that first gathering beyond the sacred Mountain.

I have lived wearied by a heavy garment of my own making ; only recently did an Angel's wisdom render me free. To finally see; that the Heavenly Plan affords no regret ,as it's Light reveals our truth.Lest we forget.

Yet should I awake and discover that this world is an illusion and finally clear the mist of confusion.To know that that which we take as reality is but a reflection of The Ultimate Reality.

With my vision thus rendered so clear; all fear, can subside and my heart can at last bear it's witness. Then perhaps I shall understand those messages I saw when I slept; why so many tears I wept.

For Love always beckoned me to cross that divide; to meet you on that side, where heartaches are so few. Where I can discover my dreams have always been of you.

Love's Lost Continent

We who yearn to set sail upon that ocean of Love
Will always turn for direction to the starry heaven above

At last we have awoken from our Earthly slumber
Illusion our heart shall no longer encumber

In our supplication we pray the hour is not too late
To orientate our soul toward Love and reverse our fate

And journey upon the emerald sea of dreams
In search of the precious stone that gleams

In the heart of our beloved to whom we were betrothed
That Time when, in innocence, our bodies were clothed

My love; in you my soul recognises Divinity immanent
In your arms my heart returns to Love's Lost Continent

The Presence of You

We have danced in each other's dreams;
For an eternity now it seems

Our truths yet only partially revealed;
Despite our protestations that our hearts have healed

Still I wait with all the patience I can muster;
Willing that Time would move just a little faster

So we can at last shed the remaining veils;
For love surely wins where everything else fails

All I desire is to offer a heart that is true;
All I desire is to offer all the love you are due;
All I desire is to offer all my joy for the Presence of You

The Real You

Today all seem to seek only Love's pleasure;
Forgetting that our sacrifice remains its true measure

I would be willing to endure any trial;
To taste that truth beyond your smile

I would be willing to shed all my tears;
To give you faith enough to unveil all your fears

I would be willing to put my soul to death;
To unite with yours for just a single breath

I beg you give me the chance to let you love anew;
For my whole heart yearns for the Real You

Heaven in One Touch

Memory insists that we must first have met in a dream;
For daily reality is rarely what it seems

Oftentimes my heart has been exposed;
In a world where darkness and light remain opposed

Then in that moment our souls first met;
My heartaches I was able to finally forget

For I knew in that instant what was true;
That I would do, anything, everything, for you.

To honour the lifetimes we had already shared;
In those realms where without fear souls are bared

If you now asked for my last breath, it would not be asking
too much;
For I know that in our "re-union" I can taste Heaven in
one touch

Love's Doorway

Forgiven are those souls that sincerely repent
Recipients of that grace which is Heaven sent

For they are empowered all veils to asunder rent
Standing proud; no longer cowering and bent

For I, my beloved, have at long last discovered
That my primordial essence can be recovered

No matter the darkness I may have known
Divine Mercy revivifies each seed of hope sown

You are the harvest of my soul's every toil
The flowering of love planted in my heart's soil

It is you always I see when I kneel daily to pray
Let us leave the past and enter Love's doorway

Love's Divine Ascent

We who have been drowned in waters of forgetfulness
Recall our desolation in distance from truthfulness

Seduced and engulfed by ephemeral allurements
Rendered naked within; despite our fine raiments

Love is never an artefact for cold hearts to manipulate
Such acts betray how the shadows lead us to derogate

Our true nature as fragments of the Eternal Light
Capable of lifting our souls to the greatest height

This Man, my Beloved, has recovered his Knightly heart
He offers it you; it's love for you forever to last

Pledging his protection and adoration on knee bent
In honour he shall carry you upon Love's Divine Ascent

Love's Lost Innocence

We who took the wrong turn at life's crossroad
Deep within have always known we cheaply sold

Our future for the promise of an illusory present
Our heart crying at each station of our descent

Into that shadowland of sorrow seemingly ceaseless
Where our futile endeavours proved so senseless

Yet through our dark night we stumbled to our light
Unsteadily blinking to reclaim our primordial right

To open our hearts fully as our tears were flowing
Within each teardrop a seed of Divine Love sowing

Until Heaven's miracle unveiled within, your presence
Such that we can forever bathe in Love's Lost innocence

Love's Glorious Quest

Would that our heart could see its Truth
Would that our wounds compassion soothe

Yet this world manifests lessons imperfectly
Often the greatest stories begin in complexity

For reasons unveiled to souls discerning
Silently we must stand as Life continues turning

In our contemplation we may see Divinity's Light
Which bestows our hearts with pristine sight

My beloved, for the longest time, I have yearned
For your return; so many lessons I have learned

For you, this Man, shall endure the greatest test
To reunite and commence Love's Glorious Quest

Love's Honour

Ahead of our next tryst patiently I purify my soul
Only in our eternal union can I become whole

Long years has my memory been seared by your eyes
Each a receptacle of every one of Heaven's signs

Yet should I ever breach my pledge of purity
Better that you banish me from you for eternity

This fate I accept if my love is ever incomplete
"Old Souls" feel the anguish of any such deceit

Fear not my love; all of my heart is yours to claim
Our union's music ensures no dance is the same

Search I shall for you in this realm's every corner
To adorn you with that love cloaked only in Honour

Love's Celestial Stations

Those who build impenetrable walls seek protection
For a heart wounded by cowardly rejection

Yet should they meet a kindred will they trust
Their soul's whispers and do what they must?

To look into the eyes of another and again search
For that Heavenly Light shining still upon Earth

And in her tears of recognition, drowning out doubt
She knows Love demands a heart pure and stout

Honouring departed souls who guide us still
Taking the hand of her Twin to follow Destiny's Will

Knowing that her Knight's heart has ceaseless patience
To carry her soul to Love's every celestial station

REUNION

There are still those of us that recall a different time; when promises made were meant to abide. When simply the glimpse of a woman's eyes remained a man's greatest prize.

When to simply share her words made men's hearts soar with the birds. When to honour, cherish and adore her, was what men understood love was meant for.

You hesitate when I offer my hand; memories of past pain, I understand. But this Man a thousand deaths would endure; for one moment with a heart which is pure.

Ceaseless sorrows he would accept; for one true kiss where our souls met. Willing to sacrifice all I have; this Man would do anything to win your hand.

Should lovers each other need? Is that not a bondage from which we should be freed? Today we are told even in love to be independent; yet so many feel alone and distant.

No my heart screams, this will not suffice! I want a love for which my very life I would sacrifice. A love for which I would be prepared; to be a fool or hero if you but dared. A love for which my very next breath would depend; upon that next kiss you may send.

Obsession

Love's Obsession

Easy it remains to reduce love to the chimerical
And seek to deride its essence in the Mystical

Few are the souls whose very look utterly transforms
Whose touch banishes the fiercest of life's storms

My Angel, you still carry the sorrow hidden in your eyes
My heart still carries the pain of so many goodbyes

Still, Time unveils the scarcity of Love in our Age
It's story reduced to myth on Life's every page

I have waited so long, my Angel, to taste your kiss
To know in each embrace our dream's eternal bliss

That which is the preserve of two hearts reunited in Creation
That they may again fulfil Love's Divine Obsession

My Last Breath

Entranced always I struggle to give expression
To the vision of you in my heart's confession

You, whose compassion and kindness inspires
Whose very voice ignites all my fires

Within the cauldron that is my very centre
Whose door is open only for you to enter

Would you trust me if I held out my hand
Would you follow me to that sacred land

Where hearts that are pure and full of honour
Can forge eternal strength in their surrender

For there my beloved we can transcend death
Even as we whisper "I love you" with my last breath

Love's Dance

In those realms where we once held one another
Did our hearts' dream of our Eden lasting forever

Only after we were placed upon our descent
To this world, did our hearts know what it meant

To suffer ; as "old souls" striving for their reunion
Two lights seeking meaning in today's confusion

Must we remain strangers in a strange land?
Yearning still for the Infinite in each other's hand

Yet search our heart must for its place of refuge
This world's shallow allures it shall always refuse

Will this world ever be prepared for our romance?
Surely our hearts can still teach it love's divine dance

Love's Release

Should we die in each moment we are separated
The beauty of our every kiss cannot be negated

For in those embraces our eyes closed tight
No longer our demons and pain we need fight

Extinguished the shadows of the past by love's light
Banished all fears each time we hold one another tight

Those departed souls upon whose memory we meditate
Their countenances' compassion guide still our Fate

All my defences crumbled; my heart in your hand
We are Reunited; two flames in one fire we stand

Weeping before you my soul finds repose in your peace
Take my hand, my Angel, and let us all our Love Release

Love's Immortality

Rarely we find the mirror of our heart in another soul
Yet search still we do for this is our true earthly goal

Weighed by the past; strewn with many wrong turns
Heaven aligns it's blessings for the heart that earns

Such a reward for retaining unshakeable faith
That it shall reunite with its Divinely twinned mate

My beloved ; I had to fall to the depths of despair
Before I recovered the lost words of my true prayer

With you, my Angel, my Spirit at last finds it's repose
Our future beckons as the present comes to a close

All true journeys lead home; where Love is our Reality
In each other's eyes we can glimpse Love's Immortality

Love's Initiation

Some truths are such that the pen cannot write
Unveiled only to those hearts touched by Divine Light

Will You guide me once more in my wretchedness
One formerly tainted by the stain of forgetfulness?

Surely the hour is not too late for my reclamation
Even one brought so low can begin his ascension

In that moment in this realm our paths crossed
Was my heart in love's pure water truly washed

You, my Angel, have brought my soul back home
As one, this kindred heart, will again never be alone

Forever I shall bathe you in all my adoration
From our first kiss we began Love's Initiation

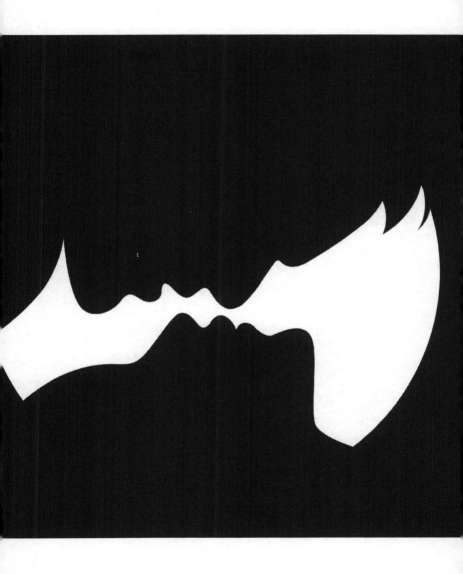

Love's Conveyance

Only for his true Angel can the poet offer his pen
He can lose in love often ; only to begin again

He can offer his charm to all but his soul to one
Many celestial bodies there are; yet just one Sun

His ardour forever a reflection of your beautiful soul
My Angel; Love remains this Man's perennial goal

It matters not how much of his heart others stole
This moment he knows for him the bell does toll

At last, my beloved, our destinies have coalesced
My heart surrendered; it's love for you confessed

Take my hand; let us hold Time itself in abeyance
Let our heart's unity become Love's true Conveyance

Love's Sacred Silence

Confess I shall to trepidation about losing you
You whose manifestation has made me live anew

So great our treasure, breathtaking our pleasure
Heaven alone knows what shall be our measure

We who have been broken and simply cast aside
Facing our moment of truth we must truly decide

To cease dreaming in slumber and start living
To cast aside self doubt and begin believing

That of your heart, my beloved, we are deserving
That in our love of you, Heaven we are serving

That our paths have crossed by Divine Guidance
That our truths are spoken in Love's Silence

Covenant of Love

Never did I imagine as I wept;
That our Divine Love was the secret Time had kept

Through all the years of my inauthenticity;
Protecting our vow made in pre-eternity

In that celestial realm, where Love always remains at the helm;
You have waited patiently

Until your heart could see;
I, at last, had journeyed back to the true me

So that we could pledge our hearts to Heaven above;
And together redeem our eternal Covenant of Love

Love's Second Perfection

We who have known the pain of Love's betrayals
Seek solace in the wisdom that Heaven never fails

To bestow Infinite Mercy upon hearts that still dream
Reality in this realm is never what it may seem

For behind all external Forms resides True Essence
Awaiting its kindred to uncover its effervescence

Long it has been written that we were born in Glory
Featured, my beloved, in the pages of every love story

In that abode of sublimity we tasted Infinity
Our souls betrothed to one another for Eternity

My Angel, in our reunion, we commence our ascension
In each other's hearts discover Love's Second Perfection

Passion

Love's Flame

We who have searched for the path to tomorrow
Know that in this realm it is time we borrow

Yet our hearts recall that our love is covenantal
Forged in Divine Disclosure and instrumental

In that renewal by which our broken world can heal
Only by the union of kindred souls can we feel

That primordial passion whose molten fire
Burns in our expression of ceaseless desire

In tracing each curve of your body I am reclaimed
Our twinned furnace of sensuality can never be tamed

Through our hearts true surrender, our world will never be
the same
Through the melting of our souls we can ignite Love's Flame

Love's Protection

We whose eyes burn in the fire of obsession
Reveal the depth of our desire in our passion

My Angel, I am lost in every kiss we share
Mesmerised completely in your every stare

Let me mark your body with crosses of Light
Our journey to forever we can no longer fight

Worthy at last to attain to love's very ecstasy
Melted hearts, we soar in our bodily unity

Eternal bonds forged in the intensity of our flame
Reuniting again; our reality shall never be the same

For Heaven's signs are unveiled in true elation
In our true surrender we gain Love's Protection

Love's Every Dimension

Together we have ventured to that Hidden Land
Somewhere only we know; hand locked in hand

Our Destiny sealed in a kiss under Love's tree
When our hearts knew what it meant to be free

Lost yet yearning; all our lives our souls ablaze
Even amidst the darkest times in Life's maze

There remained the embers of a fire lit forever
Forging a unity of Twin Souls nothing can sever

All my life I have waited for you, my beauty
In our every touch the present melts to eternity

Our reunion surpasses every poet's imagination
Our passion traverses Love's every dimension

§ 91 §

Love's Sacred Fire

Long I have waited in vain seeking ease for my pain
Regret and sorrow so often my most intimate refrain

For I am that Man within whom burns the eternal flame
That no superficiality of this world shall ever tame

Love's most ardent yearning roars in my breast
All encounters in this life are part of our true test

Shall we strive to unveil that within us which is best?
For in this realm our existence is but as a guest

You, my Angel, are the answer to my every prayer
The Twin with whom every desire I shall share

For you my passion and obsession shall never tire
Let us melt our bodies and light Love's Sacred Fire

Love's Ecstasy

True Masculinity seeks his second birth in her
She, alone, can every emotion within him stir

Not as an object as our current world insists
But as the highest Theophany; he cannot resist

Cradled in love; his desire knows no bound
In the throes of passion his Heaven is found

Upon her lips his Earthly mission is revealed
In each touch of her face his destiny is sealed

All his ardour captured in bodies entwined
No other abode will he ever seek to find

For she alone is his vessel to Eternity
His Soul's crossing assured in the moment of Ecstasy

Love's First Touch

Written in pre-Eternity; only now shall our story unfold
At this moment; that dream our hearts were told

Would manifest provided we were patient and endured
One day even broken hearts would be cured

Scarce we believed in the Majesty of Divine Destiny
Yet Faith in His Measuring Out is Life's true certainty

Accept we must the vicissitudes of Earthly existence
Heaven's Mercy is Infinite for all true penitence

In honour this Man stands before you, my beloved
In each lifetime it is your heart which he has coveted

Chivalry lives in his breast and honesty is never too much
Trembling he reclaims his Truth in Love's First Touch

Consumed by You

Were we to become lost I would wish never to be found
Were we never to speak then silence the perfect sound

When you enter the room my eyes I cannot avert
From your face so that I am again a convert

To the mythical truth that two hearts can unite
Such that their two flames entwine in one light

Which engulfs each lover into a single soul
For now, my beloved, my saviour is your Divine role

Calling us to re ignite each other's primordial fire
My desire for you across eternity will never tire

With each meeting of our lips the fire melts my heart
With each meeting of our bodies my path to heaven can start

Love's Adoration

Each Man must seek his Angel of Beauty
If he has any hope in this life to be free

Of the illusion and veils of Modernism's curse
That reduces love to mechanics or even worse

Only when I can see with the eyes of my heart
Can our souls journey in honour truly start

For it is my heart that moves the depths of my desire
To offer you a promise of passion's consuming fire

For it is my heart that makes my defences crumble
And in my nakedness before you tremble

To offer you the fruits of love without cessation
And adorn every part of you with love's endless adoration

Music of Love

We for whom earthly delights have become tasteless
Now roam in the world of our dreams restless

For that song played upon the minstrels' lute
For that melody played upon the mystics' flute

So that, my beloved, we may recover that sound
Of sacred delight; when love once lost is again found

In the ravishing of your body I can escape my hell
In the joy of ecstasy I can again hear Heaven's bell

In the summit of such surrender are we no longer blind
Only in the height of such passion can we hope to find

The theatre of Divine Love's every blessed note
And our souls upon Love's music can once again float

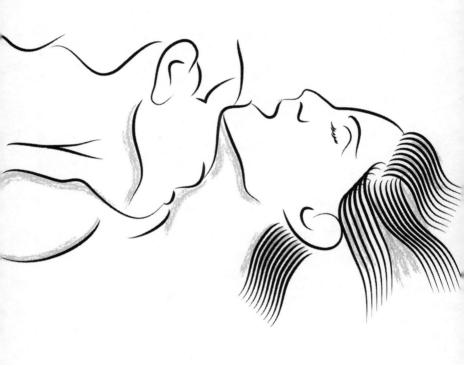

Love Letters

My heart has lived within all of Love's seasons
Yet it sees in your presence so many reasons

To believe that finally it can shed every veil
In love our self authenticity can never fail

In our truth we soar beyond this Earth
In you my soul at last finds its re birth

The hunger is revealed in each other's eyes
Love's full expression can no longer be denied

That true love is an unquenchable thirst
Every touch permitting passions to fully burst

Forever free we can cast aside all fetters
Letting our bodies compose exquisite love letters

CLOSING

Today the battle fiercely rages; perhaps the culmination of all Modern Ages.

For dominion of our souls and that of our world; lead by those who preach only division and hate. Yet this must not be our fate; for Traditional Wisdom offers the pole to which we can all cling.

In order to bring, its guiding light to this moment of time. What we seek we shall surely find. That Oneness is the central truth of all Revelation; and in that perennial message resides the source of our salvation.

For the perfected human heart can never fail; through its compassion to lift a corner of the veil. To bear witness to the truth no force can resist.

That God is Love and that Love alone does exist.

Witness to Perfection

We who seek peaceful refuge in the world of dreams
Too often have learned reality is rarely what it seems

In the sorrows of our heart we have safely placed
The pain that destiny has required we faced

In order that we prepare to finally manifest
The latent attributes that will bring out the best

Of our humanity, dignity and individual beauty
Only such vulnerability can make us truly free

To know that in our breast resides Unity of Being
That Oneness that, perhaps, our world is finally seeing

As the true message contained in each Divine emanation
In loving completely we shall witness our human perfection